Countries and

Dominican Republic

by Susan E. Haberle

Content Consultant:
Dr. Silvio Torres-Saillant
Director, Latino-Latin American Studies Program
Syracuse University
Syracuse, New York

Reading Consultant:
Dr. Robert Miller, Professor of Special Populations
Minnesota State University, Mankato

Capstone press
Mankato, Minnesota

Capstone Press
151 Good Counsel Drive, P.O. Box 669, Mankato, MN 56002
www.capstonepress.com

Copyright © 2004 by Capstone Press. All rights reserved.
No part of this publication may be reproduced in whole or in part, or stored in a retrieval system, or transmitted in any form or by any means, electronic, mechanical, photocopying, recording, or otherwise, without written permission of the publisher. For information regarding permission, write to Capstone Press, 151 Good Counsel Drive, P.O. Box 669, Mankato, Minnesota 56002.
Printed in the United States of America

Library of Congress Cataloging-in-Publication Data
Haberle, Susan E.
　Dominican Republic / by Susan E. Haberle.
　v. cm.—(Countries and cultures)
　Includes bibliographical references and index.
　Contents: Explore the Dominican Republic—The land, climate, and wildlife—The Dominican Republic's history and government—The Dominican Republic's economy—The people, culture, and daily life.
　　ISBN-10: 0-7368-2177-5 (hardcover)
　　ISBN-13: 978-0-7368-6954-6 (softcover pbk.)
　　ISBN-10: 0-7368-6954-9 (softcover pbk.)
　1. Dominican Republic—Juvenile literature. [1. Dominican Republic.]
I. Title. II. Series.
F1934.2.H33 2004
972.93—dc21　　　　　　　　　　　　　　　　　　　　　　　　　　2003002652

Summary: Discusses the geography, history, economy, and culture of the Dominican Republic.

Editorial Credits
Gillia Olson, editor; Heather Kindseth, series designer; Molly Nei, cover and interior designer; Alta Schaffer, photo researcher; Karen Risch, product planning editor

Photo Credits
Cover images: orchids, Brand X Pictures; boat anchored near shore, Corbis/Richard Bickel

Art Resource, 18, Art Resource/Reunion des Musees Nationaux, 21; Aurora/Lynn Johnson, 50–51; Aurora/Tina Soriano/Bilderberg, 47; Beryl Goldberg, 1 (right), 43; Bob Reis, 40 (25-centavo coin); Bruce Coleman Inc./Joe McDonald, 17; Bruce Coleman Inc./Kike Calvo–V&W, 1 (middle); Bruce Coleman Inc./M. Timothy O'Keefe, 8, 34; Bruce Coleman Inc./Sullivan & Rogers, 56; Capstone Press/Gary Sundermeyer, 53; Corbis, 25; Corbis/Bettmann, 27, 32; Corbis/Jeremy Horner, 4, 23; Corbis/Richard Bickel, 44; Corbis/Tom Bean, 11, 55, 63; Corbis/Tony Arruza, 13; Getty Images/Hulton Archive, 29, 30; Lynne Wies, 40 (1-peso coin); Mrs. Andres Redondo, 40 (bills and 5-peso coin); One Mile Up Inc., 57 (both); Viesti Collection Inc./Martha Cooper, 1 (left), 48; Viesti Collection Inc./Thomas Kanzler, 36

Artistic Effects
Brand X Pictures, Digital Vision, EarthStar, PhotoDisc Inc.

1 2 3 4 5 6 08 07 06 05 04 03

Contents

Chapter 1
Fast Facts about the Dominican Republic 4
Explore the Dominican Republic 5

Chapter 2
Fast Facts about the Land 8
Land, Climate, and Wildlife 9

Chapter 3
Fast Facts about History 18
The Dominican Republic's History and Government 19

Chapter 4
Fast Facts about the Economy 36
The Dominican Republic's Economy 37

Chapter 5
Fast Facts about the People 44
People, Culture, and Daily Life 45

Maps
Geopolitical Map of the Dominican Republic 7
Land Regions and Topography 15
Industries and Natural Resources 39

Features
Rhinoceros Iguana 17
The Dominican Republic's Money 40
Learn to Speak Spanish 51
Recipe: Make Helado de Coco 53
Dominican Republic's National Symbols 57
Timeline 58
Words to Know 60
To Learn More 61
Useful Addresses 62
Internet Sites 62
Index 64

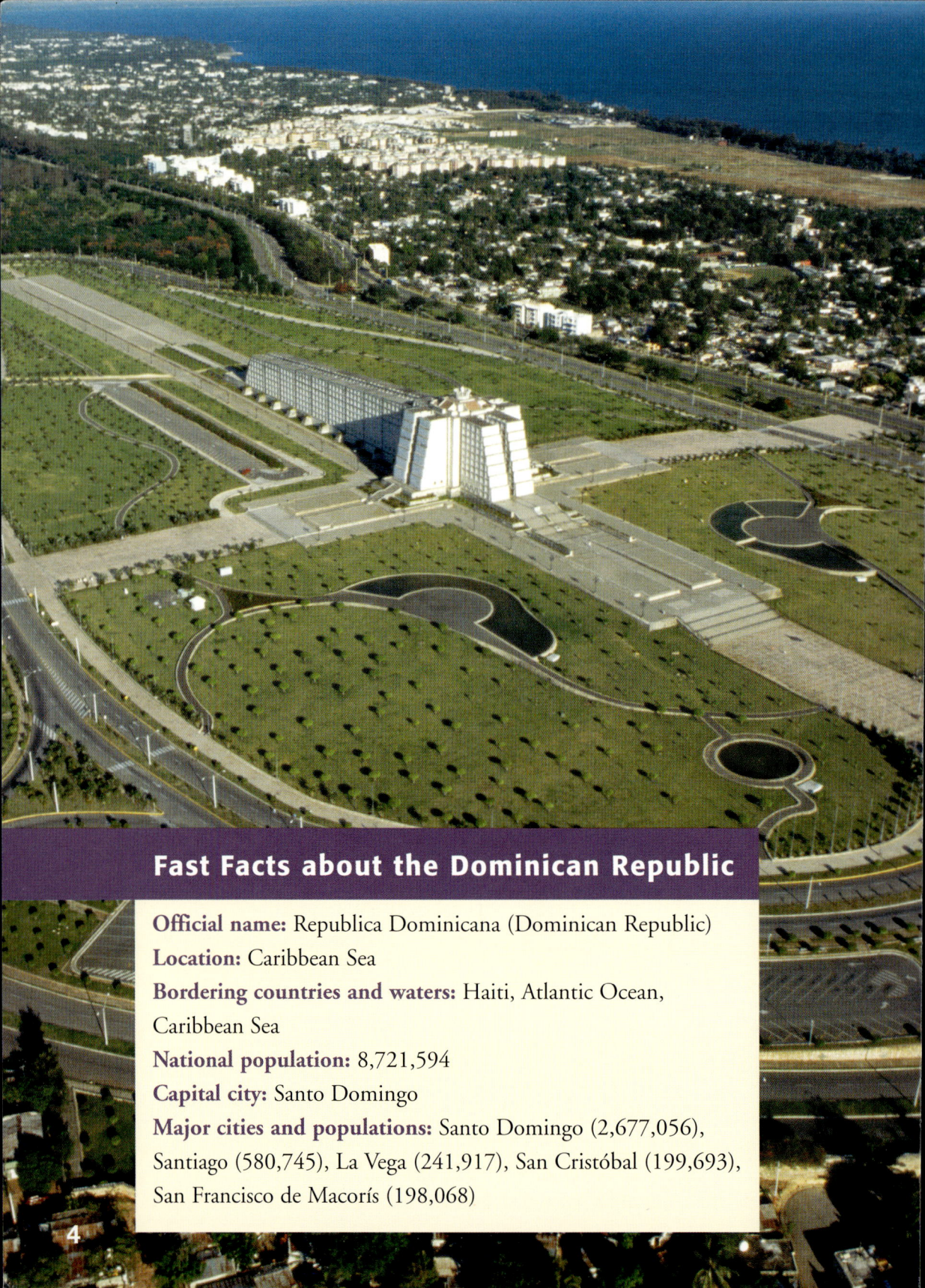

Fast Facts about the Dominican Republic

Official name: Republica Dominicana (Dominican Republic)
Location: Caribbean Sea
Bordering countries and waters: Haiti, Atlantic Ocean, Caribbean Sea
National population: 8,721,594
Capital city: Santo Domingo
Major cities and populations: Santo Domingo (2,677,056), Santiago (580,745), La Vega (241,917), San Cristóbal (199,693), San Francisco de Macorís (198,068)

Chapter 1

Explore the Dominican Republic

Christopher Columbus landed on the island of Hispaniola in 1492. He was looking for a way to travel from Europe to India without sailing around Africa. In 1992, the government of the Dominican Republic built a lighthouse to mark the 500-year anniversary of Columbus' arrival. The Columbus Lighthouse is shaped like a cross lying on the ground. Lights on the top of the building shine into the sky, forming a cross. The lights can be seen from as far away as Puerto Rico. The Columbus Lighthouse is located in the capital city of Santo Domingo.

The lighthouse stirred up controversy as it was built. To make room for it, poor people living in the area were forced to move. The lighthouse also cost about $20 million. Some people felt the money could be better spent on other projects. Often, the country does not have enough electricity even to light the

◀ The cross-shaped Columbus Lighthouse lies in a large park on Santo Domingo's coast.

beams. Other people point out that Columbus' arrival allowed the Spanish to take the land away from the island's native people.

Another controversy concerns the bones buried at the lighthouse. Some people in the Dominican Republic say that Columbus' remains are at the lighthouse. Others believe his remains are in Spain.

The Dominican Republic

The Dominican Republic is located in the West Indies. This group of islands rims the Caribbean Sea between Florida and South America. The Dominican Republic shares the island of Hispaniola with Haiti. Haiti is on the western one-third of the island, while the Dominican Republic is on the eastern two-thirds.

Besides Haiti, the Dominican Republic borders the Atlantic Ocean and the Caribbean Sea. The countries closest to Hispaniola are Cuba and Puerto Rico. Cuba is about 50 miles (80 kilometers) to the northwest, while Puerto Rico is about 60 miles (97 kilometers) to the east. A waterway called the Mona Passage runs between the Dominican Republic and Puerto Rico.

The Dominican Republic is the second largest country in the Caribbean. Only Cuba is larger. The Dominican Republic covers 18,657 square miles (48,322 square kilometers) of land. It is about the size of the U.S. states of New Hampshire and Vermont combined.

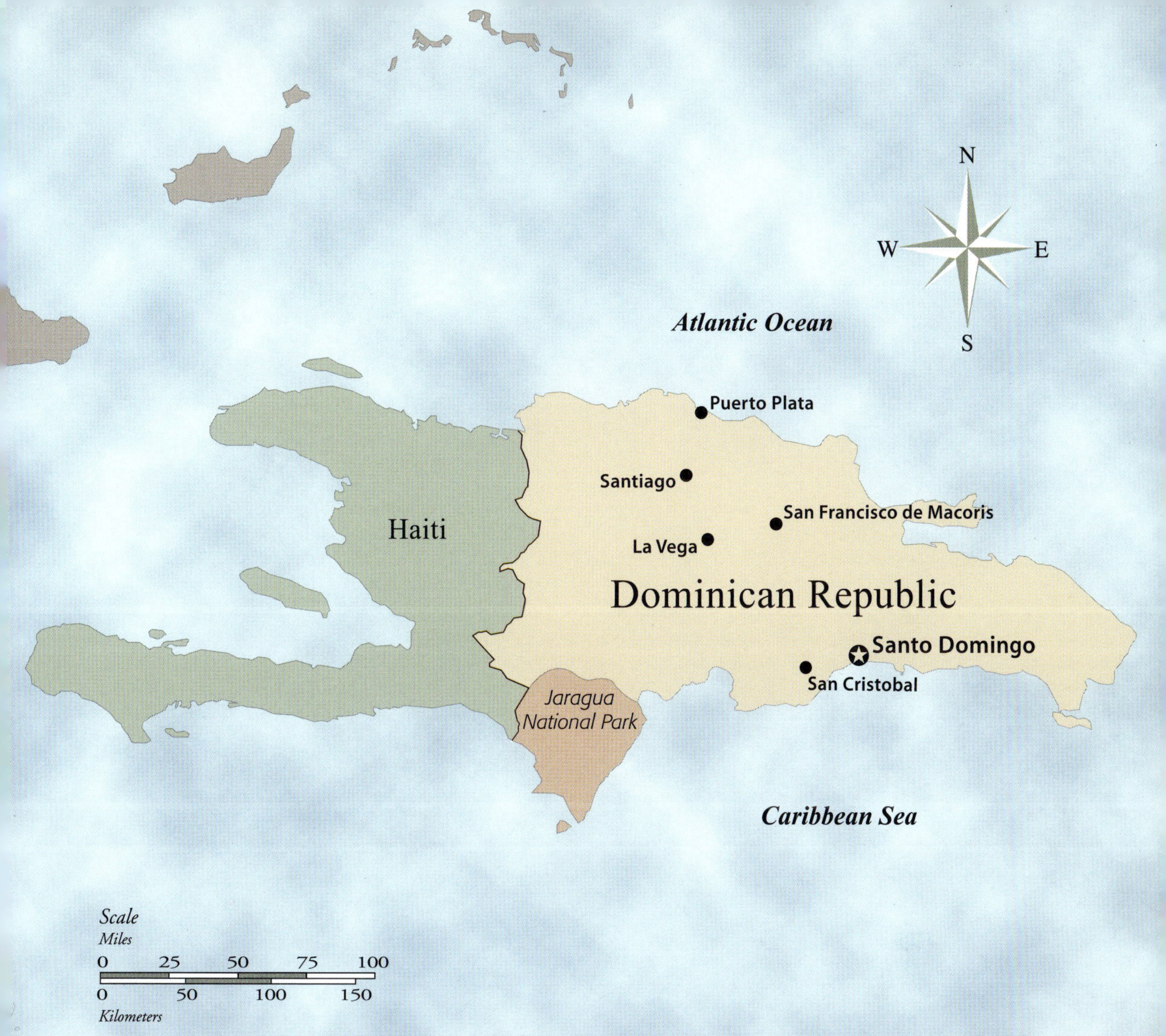

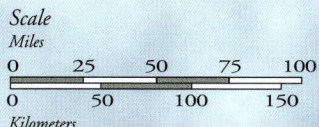

Geopolitical Map of the Dominican Republic

KEY
- ✪ Capital
- ● City
- ▭ National Park

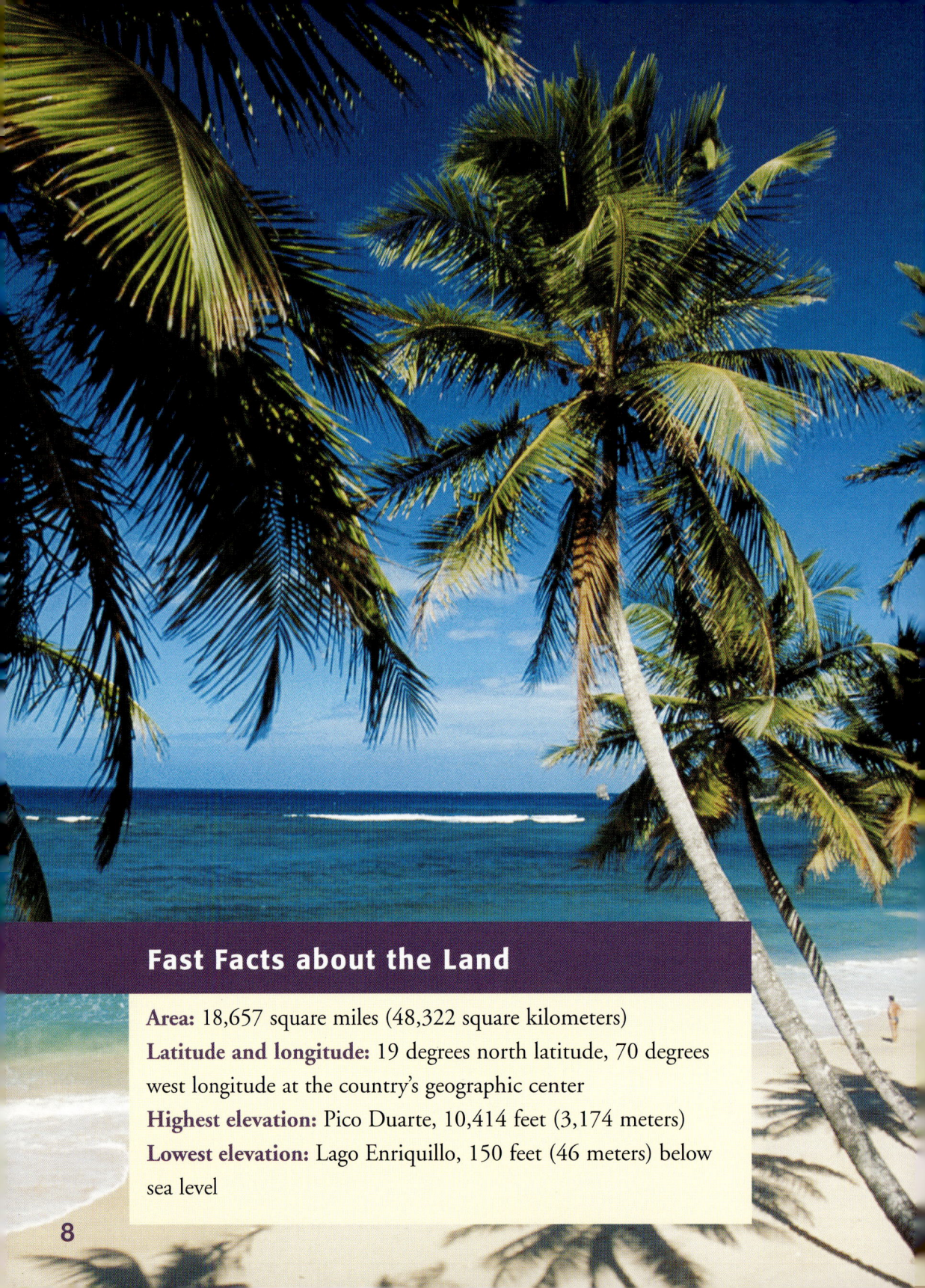

Fast Facts about the Land

Area: 18,657 square miles (48,322 square kilometers)
Latitude and longitude: 19 degrees north latitude, 70 degrees west longitude at the country's geographic center
Highest elevation: Pico Duarte, 10,414 feet (3,174 meters)
Lowest elevation: Lago Enriquillo, 150 feet (46 meters) below sea level

Chapter 2

Land, Climate, and Wildlife

Mountains cover about 80 percent of the Dominican Republic. The four major ranges are the Cordillera Septentrional, the Cordillera Central, the Sierra de Neiba, and the Sierra de Bahoruco. These mountain ranges help divide the country into the northern, central, and southwestern regions.

The Northern Region

The northern region contains the Atlantic coastal plain and the Samaná Peninsula. The Dominican Republic has a long, beautiful coastline. Beaches in the northern region and around the rest of the country attract many tourists. Tourists also enjoy the beautiful coral reefs along the northern coastline.

Puerto Plata is the center of tourism in the northern region. Many resorts are located here along beautiful beaches. Puerto Plata is located near an area

◀ White sand beaches attract tourists to the Dominican Republic's north coast.

9

> **Did you know...?**
> Sometimes, when sap ran down a tree trunk millions of years ago, insects got trapped in it. As the sap hardened into amber, the insects were preserved. The world's oldest insect is trapped in amber from the Dominican Republic.

called the Amber Coast. Hardened tree sap, called amber, is found here. The tree sap that formed amber is millions of years old. The yellowish-brown material can be polished and used in jewelry.

The Cordillera Septentrional and the Cibao Valley are also located in the northern region. The Cordillera Septentrional runs parallel to the coastal plain. The fertile Cibao Valley lies south of the mountain range. The Dominican Republic's second largest city, Santiago, is located in the Cibao Valley.

The Central Region

The largest mountain range in the Dominican Republic is the Cordillera Central. It runs through the middle of the country. The highest mountain in the West Indies, Pico Duarte, is in this range. It is 10,414 feet (3,174 meters) above sea level. An offshoot of these mountains, the Cordillera Oriental, starts near the Rio Ozama and runs eastward almost to the coast.

Major rivers start in the Cordillera Central. Rio Yaque del Norte runs from Pico Duarte to the sea. It

▼ Rio Yaque del Norte begins in the Cordillera Central.

supplies water to Santiago and irrigates farms in the Cibao Valley. Rio Yaque del Sur, Rio Camu, and Rio Ozama also begin in Cordillera Central and run to the sea.

Santo Domingo, the capital of the Dominican Republic, is located in the central region. It was the first Spanish capital in the Americas. The first university, the first cathedral, and the first castle in the Americas are in Santo Domingo. Today, Santo Domingo is the cultural center of the country.

The Southwestern Region

The Sierra de Neiba and Sierra de Bahoruco are two mountain ranges in the southwestern region. The Neiba Valley is a fertile area between the ranges where many farms are located.

Between the Sierra de Neiba and Sierra de Bahoruco lies a large geographic depression. The largest of the Dominican Republic's few lakes is in this depression. Lago Enriquillo is larger than Manhattan Island in New York and three times saltier than the ocean. It is the lowest point in the West Indies, at 150 feet (46 meters) below sea level.

Jaragua National Park is on the southern tip of the southwestern region. It is the largest park in the country. The park includes two islands, Isla Beata and Isla Alto Velo. Flamingos and sea turtles nest in the park. Isla Beata contains 26 types of reptiles and

▲ A view from a cave shows Lago Enriquillo and its surrounding desertlike environment.

amphibians that live only on the island. The park also has beautiful beaches.

The Climate

The Dominican Republic has a tropical climate. The temperature stays nearly the same throughout the year. In January, the average temperature is 75 degrees

Fahrenheit (24 degrees Celsius). In July, the average is 81 degrees Fahrenheit (27 degrees Celsius). Along the coast and in the valleys, the temperature can reach 100 degrees Fahrenheit (38 degrees Celsius). Temperatures in the cooler mountains can dip below freezing.

The Dominican Republic has two seasons. The dry season runs from December to April. The rainy season lasts from May through November. Many storms, including hurricanes, can happen during the rainy season.

Large hurricanes have damaged the Dominican Republic in recent years. In 1979, Hurricane David killed 2,000 people in Santo Domingo. In 1998, Hurricane Georges killed more than 200 people and left more than 170,000 homeless. Large sections of forest were destroyed. Tourism was hurt because of the damage to natural areas.

Plant Life

Plant life in the Dominican Republic varies with the climate. Pine forests cover the cool, high altitudes of the Cordillera Central. Cactuses grow in dry areas in the southwest. Mahogany, ebony, guava, cashew, and mangrove trees grow in the rain forests on the lower slopes of the mountains. A wide variety of

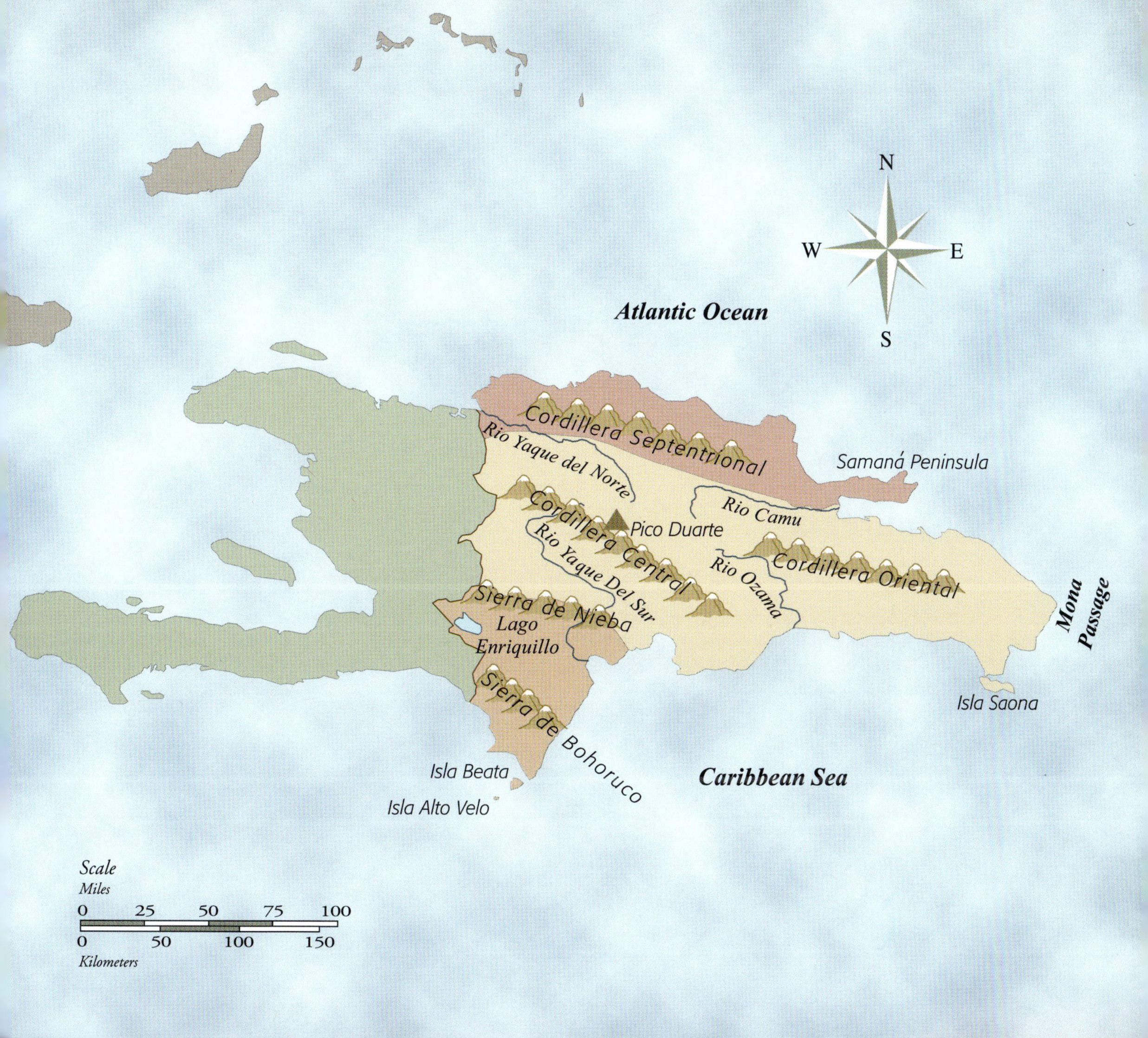

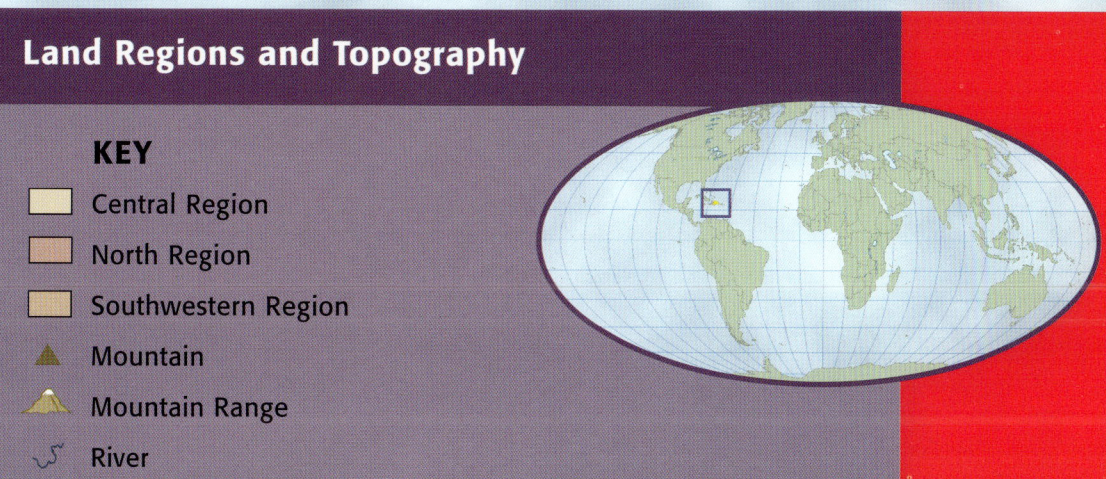

Land Regions and Topography

KEY
- Central Region
- North Region
- Southwestern Region
- ▲ Mountain
- Mountain Range
- River

orchids and other flowers grow throughout the island. Palm trees shade the beaches.

Some of the Dominican Republic's best-known plants were brought by settlers for use in farming. Europeans brought sugarcane, coffee, and bananas. Citrus fruits and cacao plants came from Central and South America.

Animals

The warm ocean waters around the Dominican Republic are home to a huge variety of life. Crabs, shrimp, oysters, red snapper, sardines, eels, parrotfish, and barracuda live in the waters. Humpback whales, dolphins, and manatees swim off Samaná Bay.

Lago Enriquillo is a unique habitat. Its salty waters are home to crocodiles, turtles, and other reptiles. The rhinoceros iguana, native to the Dominican Republic, lives near the lake. Pink flamingos wade along its shore.

Many small mammals live in the Dominican Republic. Two rodents, the solendon and hutía, are endangered. The solendon looks like an anteater. The hutía looks somewhat like a guinea pig.

Rhinoceros Iguana

The rhinoceros iguana is a reptile native to the island of Hispaniola. It lives mostly in the southwestern region of the Dominican Republic. The rhinoceros iguana's olive or gray skin blends in with its dry, rocky surroundings. It gets its name from the stubby growths on its nose that are similar to a rhinoceros' horn. These lizards can grow to 4 feet (1.2 meters) long and weigh up to 22 pounds (10 kilograms).

The iguana is most active during the day. The cold-blooded reptile suns itself on rocks to warm up. After warming up, it searches for food. It eats fruit, leaves, and sometimes insects or eggs. It spends the night in a burrow, cave, or other shelter.

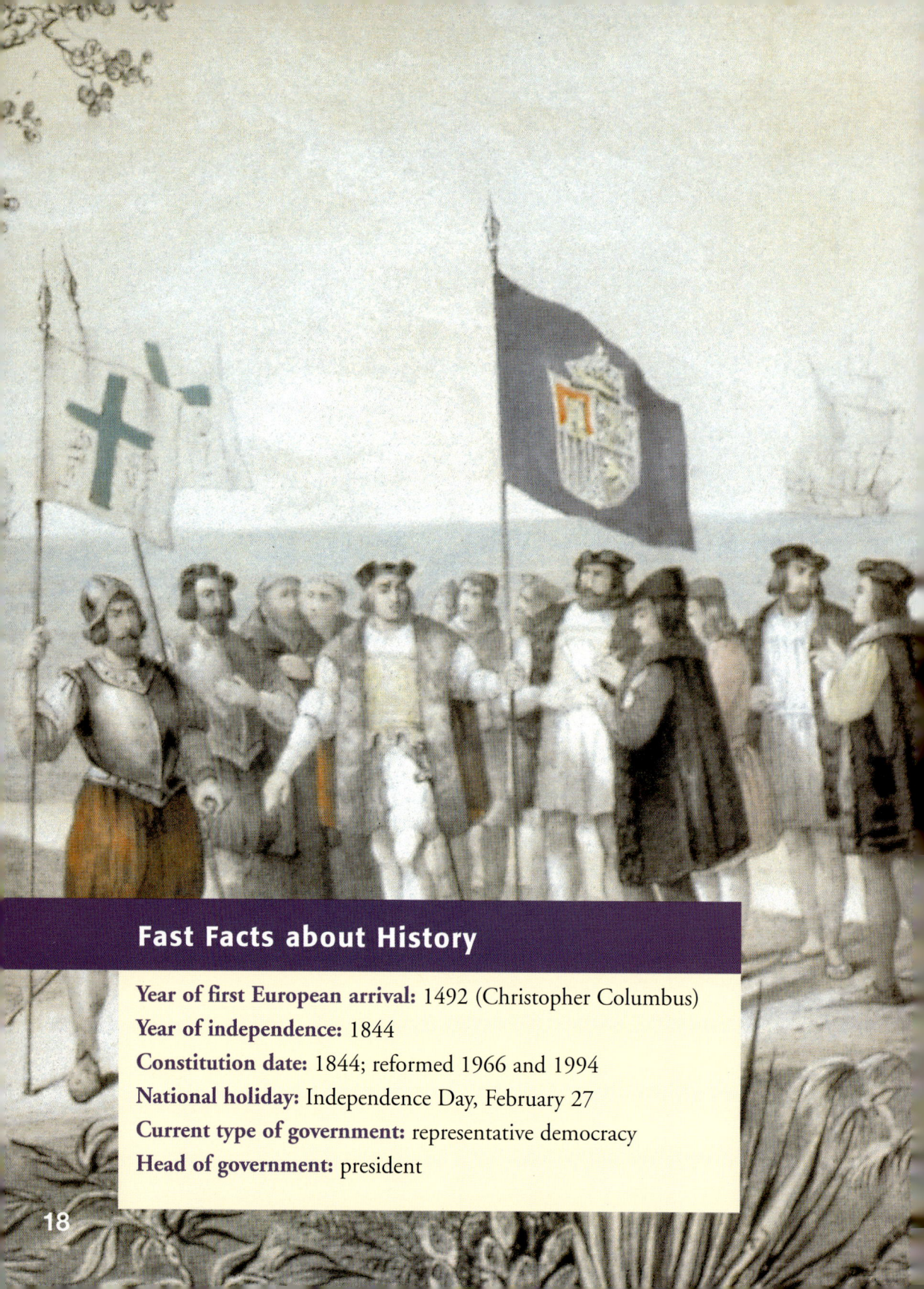

Fast Facts about History

Year of first European arrival: 1492 (Christopher Columbus)
Year of independence: 1844
Constitution date: 1844; reformed 1966 and 1994
National holiday: Independence Day, February 27
Current type of government: representative democracy
Head of government: president

Chapter 3

The Dominican Republic's History and Government

The earliest settlers on Hispaniola were the Taíno (ty-EE-no). Their ancestors were Arawaks who came by canoe from South America between 4000 and 3000 B.C. The Taíno planted sweet potatoes, corn, cotton, and tobacco. They also hunted and fished to feed their families.

Spanish Rule

In A.D. 1492, while searching for a trade route across the Atlantic Ocean, Christopher Columbus landed on Cuba and Hispaniola. The Spanish were very interested in the gold the Taíno had. The Spanish founded several towns on Hispaniola. The first permanent European settlement in the Americas was Santo Domingo on Hispaniola.

Increasing numbers of Spanish settlers arrived throughout the 1500s. They claimed land and hired

◀ Christopher Columbus landed on Hispaniola in 1492.

the Taíno to work long hours in mines and on large farms. The Taíno were paid little and eventually became slaves.

The Spanish also carried diseases. The Taíno had no natural bodily defenses to the diseases, and most of them died. To replace them, the Spanish brought slaves from Africa to work in the fields and the mines.

Threats to Spanish Rule

During the late 1500s, Spain somewhat ignored Hispaniola. Spain concentrated on colonies in Central and South America where it could mine more gold. Pirates and settlers from other countries began to influence trade in Hispaniola. Pirates stole and traded goods illegally. The French began to trade heavily with Hispaniola. France established colonies in Hispaniola, especially along the western coast.

The Spanish and French fought for power in the Americas. In 1697, Spanish and French leaders signed the Treaty of Ryswick. The French kept the western third of Hispaniola, which they had been occupying. This French colony became Saint Domingue. It later became the country of Haiti.

Saint Domingue was France's most important colony. It provided much of France's goods from the New World. When French landowners needed more

▼ France created large sugar plantations in Saint Domingue.

people to work on the plantations, they brought slaves from Africa. By 1790, more than 90 percent of the people in Saint Domingue were slaves.

The Fight for Independence
African slaves from Saint Domingue led a revolt against the French landowners in 1791. Led by Toussaint Louverture, the slaves were successful.

21

> **Did you know...?**
> On the date of the Dominican revolution against Haiti, Juan Pablo Duarte was out of the country and too ill to travel. He arrived a few weeks after the revolution.

France declared Louverture governor general of Saint Domingue.

In 1795, Spain gave its remaining two-thirds of Hispaniola to France in the Treaty of Basel. Louverture entered Spanish-speaking Santo Domingo in 1801 to enforce the treaty. In theory, France now controlled all of Hispaniola, but it had little real power there.

In 1809, Spain again took control of Santo Domingo. Soon, the people of Santo Domingo grew angry with Spanish rule. The colonists declared themselves independent of Spain.

Santo Domingo no longer had Spain to defend it. In 1822, Haiti's president decided to take control of the entire island. This rule lasted for 21 years and caused mistrust between the two countries.

Juan Pablo Duarte led the Dominican Republic to independence. In 1838, he organized a revolutionary group to remove the Haitian government from Santo Domingo. Francisco del Rosario Sánchez and Ramón Mella actually led the final takeover of Santo Domingo on February 27, 1844. The country then became the Dominican Republic.

▲ A monument in Santo Domingo holds the remains of Duarte, Sánchez, and Mella.

Dictators

Though Duarte and his group wanted free elections, they were unable to accomplish this goal. Soon after independence, the general of the new Dominican army, Pedro Santana, took control of the country. Saying he needed to make quick decisions in the continuing conflict with Haiti, Santana gave himself almost unlimited power. He inserted an article in the constitution that gave the office of the president full control. Duarte, Sánchez, and Mella were imprisoned and eventually forced to leave the country.

In 1849, Buenaventura Báez won the election for president. Santana and Báez competed for power for more than a decade. Control of the country switched back and forth between them.

Spanish Annexation

Both Santana and Báez thought the best defense for the Dominican Republic was to combine with a foreign country. At one time or another, Spain, France, and the United States were asked to protect the Dominican Republic. In 1861, Santana asked Spain to annex, or take control of, the Dominican Republic. Spain agreed. Santana became the "captain general" of the Spanish province of Santo Domingo.

Although Santana thought he had wide public support for annexation, he was mistaken. Almost immediately after Spain took control, the people of Santo Domingo revolted against the foreign government. In 1863, leaders of the revolution declared an "act of independence." The revolt against Spain became known as the War of Restoration. The Dominican Republic won the war in 1865.

◀ Pedro Santana led a campaign to make the Dominican Republic part of Spain again.

Politics and U.S. Involvement

After the revolt, conservatives in the south and liberals in the north formed separate political parties. Power struggles between the parties continued for the next 40 years. Candidates often cheated during elections. Leadership of the country changed more than 40 times between 1864 and 1905.

The country faced economic problems as well as political problems. The country's money was nearly worthless. Leaders borrowed money from other countries to pay for the military and for railroads, telegraph systems, and other improvements.

The United States' interest in Caribbean nations led it to become involved in the Dominican Republic's finances. Foreign countries, many in Europe, wanted their loans repaid. The United States did not want European involvement in the Caribbean. It also wanted the freedom to sail through the Caribbean to the Panama Canal, which was being built at this time.

In 1905, the Dominican Republic agreed to the U.S. plan of assuming control of Dominican customs. By doing so, the United States collected taxes on goods exported out of and imported into the country. With this money, the United States repaid the money the Dominican Republic owed to other countries.

U.S. Occupation

The Dominican Republic continued to be politically unstable. Political parties continued to fight with one another. Candidates cheated in elections, and leaders could not maintain power. The United States became increasingly involved with the country.

▼ U.S. Marines ride into Santo Domingo during the U.S. occupation in 1916.

In 1916, the United States sent troops into the Dominican Republic. U.S. leaders said they wanted to help the country become successful. Most Dominicans did not like a foreign power taking control of their country. While the United States built roads, schools, and hospitals, it also taxed the people, and censored radio and newspapers. Some Dominicans supported the Gavilleros, a resistance movement that formed to push out U.S. forces.

The people of the Dominican Republic wanted their freedom, and U.S. people wanted the occupation to end. When the U.S. occupation ended in 1924, U.S. leaders required that the Dominican Republic hold fair elections. Horacio Vásquez was elected president. After the United States left, the economy continued to improve.

Trujillo Era

Soon after Vásquez's election, political problems resumed in the Dominican Republic. Vásquez lengthened the term of president from four to six years. Many thought he would try to become a dictator. Fighting followed. The instability gave General Rafael Leonidas Trujillo the chance he needed to gain power. Trujillo was general of the National Army, a military force created by the United States during the occupation. As general, Trujillo had the most powerful group in the country supporting him.

Trujillo was "elected" for the first time in 1930. No one else was on the election ballot. He basically ruled until 1961. During parts of that time, his brother and other leaders were elected president, but Trujillo held the power behind the scenes.

▲ Rafael Trujillo (center) stands with his wife and daughter.

The economy did grow stronger under Trujillo's rule, but most people did not benefit. Trujillo placed most of the country's industries under the control of the government. Since Trujillo controlled government, he, his family, and his friends became rich.

Most Dominicans, and people around the world, remember Trujillo's rule as a time of terror. He imprisoned, tortured, and killed people who

▼ Dominicans demonstrate against the U.S. invasion of 1965.

opposed his rule. In 1937, he ordered the murder of Haitians living in the Dominican Republic as revenge for the killing of spies he sent to Haiti. More than 20,000 people were killed.

Trujillo was suspicious of liberal leaders in countries like Cuba and Venezuela. World leaders reduced relations with the Dominican Republic because of Trujillo's increasingly controlling and paranoid behavior. He even tried to have the president of Venezuela killed. Resistance groups formed to oppose his rule. Trujillo was assassinated in 1961.

After Trujillo

Although democratic elections were held in 1962, the military overthrew the new government seven months later. In 1965, an armed rebellion emerged to restore the constitutionally elected president. Soon after, the U.S. government sent 20,000 soldiers to stop the rebellion.

Elections were again held in 1966. Joaquín Balaguer, the U.S.-supported candidate, won the presidency. He had been a president during Trujillo's time, under the control of the dictator. Although not as controlling as Trujillo, Balaguer did use his security force to stop people who opposed his government. Balaguer was reelected in 1970 and 1974. Many people believe he won by election fraud and by threatening his opponents. Opponents dropped out of the race close to the election, fearing imprisonment or worse by Balaguer's security force.

Although fair elections were held in 1978, the country continued to face government corruption and unfair elections. Antonio Guzmán was elected in 1978. He killed himself during his last year in office, possibly

▶ In total, Joaquín Balaguer served as president of the Dominican Republic for a little more than 23 years.

due to the corruption charges against family members. Salvador Jorge Blanco, elected in 1982, faced charges of corruption from Balaguer. Balaguer was elected president in 1986. Blanco was later cleared of charges. Balaguer was reelected in 1990 and 1994, amid charges of election fraud. Most experts agreed the 1994 elections were unfair, and Balaguer agreed to step down in 1996.

The 1996 and 2000 elections appear to have been free and open. Democracy is finally starting to flourish. Dominicans are hopeful that government will remain free. Still, they will continue to watch government officials for corruption.

Government

Today, the Dominican Republic is a representative democracy. All citizens 18 years and older are required to vote. Married people younger than age 18 are also required to vote. People can receive fines for not voting. Members of the military and the police cannot vote.

Governors, who are appointed by the president, head each of the country's 31 provinces. Provinces are divided into communes, and the communes are divided into townships. Township leaders are elected by the people.

The national government has three branches. The president and a 15-person cabinet form the executive branch. The Senate and the Chamber of Deputies are the legislative branch, or the National Congress. The judicial branch includes the nine-member Supreme Court of Justice and lower courts.

▲ The National Palace holds the president's office and other government offices.

The president of the Dominican Republic is very powerful. The president appoints cabinet members and other key members of government. The cabinet is a group of advisers representing education, health care, finance, and other government agencies. The president and vice president are elected to four-year terms. They cannot be reelected.

Members of the National Congress are elected to four-year terms. The National Congress election is separate from the presidential election. The National Congress is made up of the Senate and Chamber of Deputies. The Senate includes 32 members, one member from each province and one from Santo Domingo. Population determines the number of seats in the Chamber of Deputies. In the 2002 election, the Chamber of Deputies had 150 members. Senators and deputies are elected directly by the people.

Fast Facts about the Economy

Major natural resources: ferronickel, bauxite, gold, silver
Major agricultural products: sugarcane, coffee, cotton, tobacco
Major manufactured products: cement, sugar, beer
Major exports: ferronickel, sugar, gold, silver, coffee, tobacco
Major imports: food, oil, cotton, pharmaceuticals, chemicals

Chapter 4

The Dominican Republic's Economy

Until recently, the Dominican Republic's economy was based on agriculture. Farmers grew sugarcane, coffee, and cacao for export. They also grew food to feed their families or to trade for needed items. Today, the majority of Dominicans hold service jobs in government, education, tourism, and other areas.

Agriculture

About 57 percent of the Dominican Republic's land is used for farming. Large companies and the government own about 75 percent of the farmland. Individual farmers own the rest. Individual farmers' plots of land are usually small. Farming is not easy. Farmers usually have little fertilizer, few tractors, and few irrigation tools to water the land.

Sugar is the country's largest agricultural export product. Sugar is made from sugarcane. Most

◀ Sugarcane plantation workers stack sugarcane on carts.

Dominicans will not work in the cane fields because of the low pay and poor living conditions. The majority of the workers are Haitians, who work 12 to 15 hours a day.

Dominicans raise a variety of other crops and livestock for export and for their own use. Major export products include coffee, cacao, tobacco, fruits, nuts, and spices. Cacao beans are used to make chocolate. Dominicans grow rice, corn, guavas, and plantains to feed their families. Plantains look like bananas but taste like potatoes. Farmers also raise poultry, pigs, and cattle.

Manufacturing and Free-Trade Zones

The Dominican Republic's manufacturing industry continues to grow. Some factories depend on agriculture, including sugar refineries and cigar manufacturers. Dominicans also make clothing, cement, and electronics.

The Dominican Republic has more than 30 free-trade zones. In these zones, companies do not have to pay taxes or duties on imported goods. All the companies have to do is make export products out of the imported goods. The Dominican Republic uses these zones to encourage foreign corporations to move there. U.S. businesses own two-thirds of the companies in the free-trade zones.

Industries and Natural Resources

KEY
- coffee
- gold
- livestock
- manufacturing
- nickel
- rice
- sugarcane
- tobacco

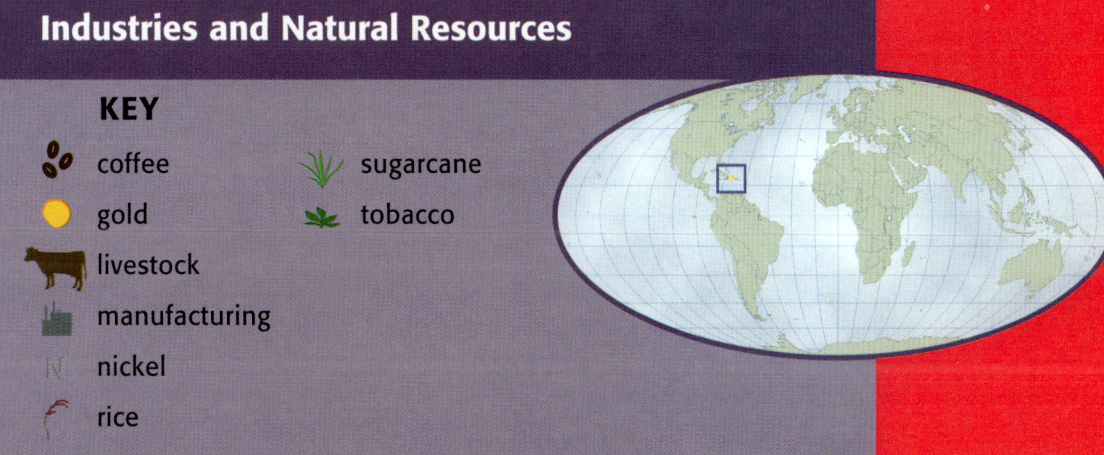

39

The Dominican Republic's Money

The Dominican Republic peso is the country's currency. One peso equals 100 centavos.

Exchange rates can change daily. In early 2003, 1 U.S. dollar equaled 21.65 pesos and 1 Canadian dollar equaled 14.62 pesos.

25 centavo coin

20 peso bill

100 peso bill

5 peso coin

1 peso coin

10 peso bill

40

Free-trade zones have advantages and disadvantages. They provide new jobs. They bring technology to the country. The foreign companies pay wages and rent. Unfortunately, they do not hire many workers, and the wages are low.

Mining and Energy

Minerals bring in the most money to the Dominican Republic, but only a small percent of the people work in the mines. Dominicans mine ferronickel, gold, iron, copper, bauxite, and doré. Bauxite is used to make aluminum. Doré is a gold and silver mixture.

Gold and nickel are the largest exports. The Pueblo Viejo mine in the middle of the country is the largest open-pit gold mine in the Western Hemisphere. In the late 1980s, the ferronickel mine in Bonao was the second largest in the world.

The Dominican Republic government struggles to meet the country's energy needs. It imports all of its oil. This oil is expensive and hard to get. Many rural areas are not connected to a power supply. Rural Dominicans often use wood for cooking and heating their homes. In cities, too little electricity is generated. Power outages happen often. The country continues to add new equipment to improve the supply of energy

> **Did you know...?**
> More than 2.8 million people visited the Dominican Republic in 2002. Residents of the United States, Canada, and France visited the most, in that order.

and to develop other sources of energy.

Tourism and Transportation

The tourism industry in the Dominican Republic is growing. The government began to promote tourism aggressively in 1971. Today, some people credit the country's economic success in large part to the increase in tourism.

Tourists come to the Dominican Republic to enjoy the wildlife and beaches. They visit La Romana, Puerto Plata, and other popular resort cities. The beautiful coral reefs and forested mountains bring ecotourists. These people try to view wildlife without disturbing animals or habitats.

The transportation system has grown with the increase in tourism. Most of the roads are paved, but they are narrow and heavily traveled. The country has five international airports. It also has one of the longest railroad systems in the Caribbean. The country has 14 ports. Santo Domingo, the largest port, handles 80 percent of the country's imports.

▼ A woman sets a table in a restaurant that caters to tourists. She is part of the country's large tourism industry.

43

Fast Facts about the People

Population distribution: 65 percent urban, 35 percent rural
Official language: Spanish
Population growth rate: 1.61 percent
Life expectancy: men—71 years, women—76 years
Literacy rate: 82.1 percent of Dominicans age 15 and older can read and write

Chapter 5

People, Culture, and Daily Life

The Dominican Republic's Taíno, Spanish, and African cultures have combined to produce a complex, modern society. While the Taíno people died out soon after the Spanish arrived, their influence lives on in Dominican life. Spanish and African influences can be seen in all aspects of Dominican culture.

The Dominican Republic has three main ethnic groups. About 16 percent of the country's people have European ancestors, mainly Spanish. People of African ancestry make up about 11 percent of the population. People of mixed African and European ancestry make up 73 percent of the population.

People from many other countries also live in the Dominican Republic. More than 200,000 Haitians live in the country. People from eastern, southern and western Asia also have moved there.

◀ A man sells paintings by local artists. The paintings show the influence of Spanish and African cultures.

Religion

The Spanish introduced the Roman Catholic religion to Hispaniola in the 1500s. During Trujillo's leadership, it was the official religion. Today, the constitution separates religion and government.

The Roman Catholic Church continues to play a large role in the country. About 95 percent of Dominicans consider themselves Catholic. Churches manage many of the country's hospitals, clinics, orphanages, nursing homes, and schools.

A large portion of the people practice religious beliefs influenced by Africans, Catholics, and natives, called vodou. People who practice vodou usually believe in a supreme god and smaller gods. While many Dominicans who practice vodou are from Haiti, scholars have identified a Dominican form of vodou.

Some Dominicans practice other religions. Protestants make up about 2 percent of the people. A very small group of Dominicans practices Judaism. Most of these people live in Sosúa. They came from Europe during World War II (1939–1945) to escape oppression and possibly death during Nazi rule.

Festivals and Holidays

Most Dominican holidays revolve around Catholicism. Christmas is celebrated throughout all of December.

▲ People often dress in wild costumes when celebrating Carnival.

On Christmas Eve, many families roast pork and have dinner with their relatives. They also attend church.

In February or March, Dominicans celebrate Carnival. It is a week of fun and feasting before the Christian period of Lent. People wear large, colorful masks and costumes. Cities hold parades with floats and marching bands. The holiday is similar to Mardi Gras in New Orleans, Louisiana.

▼ Family members of several generations gather for a meal.

Family Life and Roles

Family is important to Dominicans. Relatives often live near each other. Family members depend on each other in times of need for money, child care, or other help. Family members who have left the Dominican Republic often send money home to their families.

As in most nations around the world, men have most of the political and economic power in the Dominican Republic. Women usually add greatly to the family income, but they usually earn less than men. In farming families, women plant and tend crops and livestock. Many women work in manufacturing jobs. Many companies hire women because they will work for less pay than men.

> **Did you know...?**
> Some Dominicans believe that people's ghosts bathe in empty water containers after they die.

Children's roles usually vary depending on the wealth of their families. Most children spend their days as children in the United States and Europe do. Children of the poor sometimes need to help earn money for the family. These children sometimes sell newspapers, shine shoes, or sell flowers for extra money.

Housing

Increasingly, people of the Dominican Republic are moving to cities. In 1960, 30 percent of Dominicans lived in urban areas. In 2000, 65 percent of Dominicans lived in cities.

People in the Dominican Republic live like people in other countries. They live in the type of house or apartment that they can afford. Upper- and middle-class people often live in houses or city apartments. Often, the poor are forced to live in crowded neighborhoods of small shacks, called barrios. Barrios often do not have running water.

Health Care

Some areas of the Dominican Republic have conditions that contribute to poor health. Open sewers and unclean drinking water hold diseases. Many poor people, especially children, lack a proper diet.

Most people in the Dominican Republic use modern health care, but some believe in folk remedies. They seek advice from healers known as curanderos (koo-rahn-DAY-rohs) or brujos (BROO-hohs). People believe these healers drive out bad spirits by using herbs, roots, and home remedies.

Education

By law, children must attend primary school from ages 7 to 14. Only 70 percent usually do so. The Dominican government lacks the resources to enforce this law completely.

A variety of factors keep people from going to school. Schools are crowded. Few schools exist in rural areas. Some children must work to help the family and cannot attend school. Some families cannot afford the supplies needed to send children to school. Despite these problems, most families know that a good education will greatly improve their children's chance of success in life.

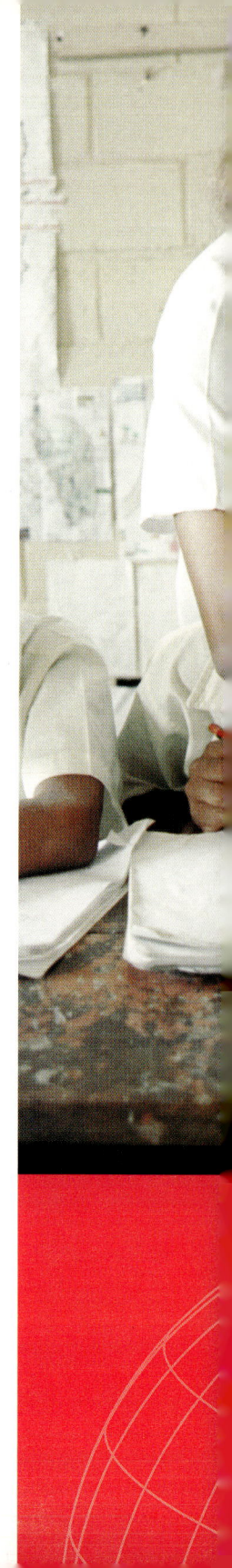

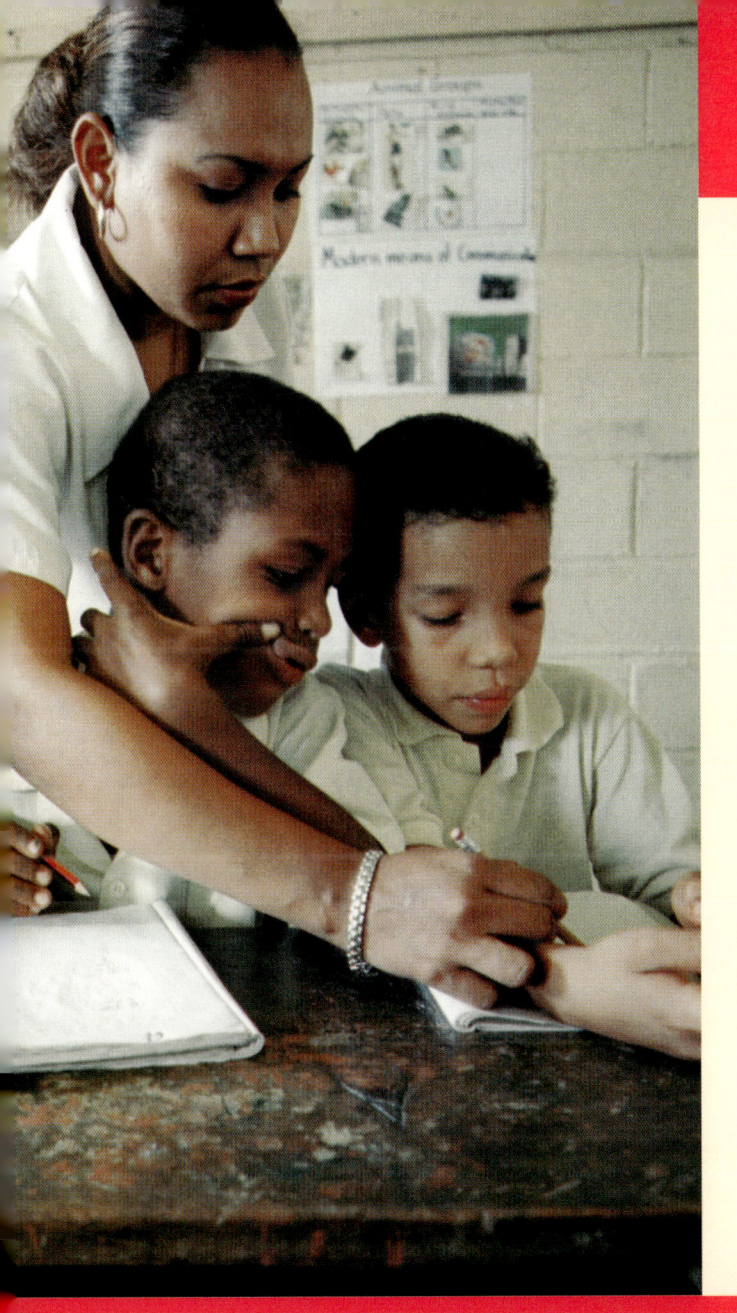

Learn to Speak Spanish

Spanish is the official language of the Dominican Republic. Below are some helpful Spanish words and phrases.

How are you?—
    Familiar: ¿Cómo estás?
    (KOH-moh eh-STASS)
    Formal: ¿Cómo está usted?
    (KOH-moh eh-STA oo-STED)
hello—hola (OH-la)
please—por favor
    (PORE fuh-VORE)
thank you—gracias
    (GRAH-see-uhs)
Do you speak English?—¿Hablas inglés? (AH-blahs in-GLAYS)

▲ Dominicans learn to write and read Spanish in school.

Fewer than half of the children attend secondary school, but most of those students go on to college. The country has 27 universities. The only public university is the Autonomous University of Santo Domingo. Wealthy families often send their children to private Christian schools or to schools in the United States and Europe.

Food

Most Dominicans have access to a wide variety of foods. Tuna, salmon, and shark are popular. Dominicans also enjoy plantains, papaya, mango, coconut, guava and other tropical fruits.

Lunch is the largest meal of the day. This meal usually includes beans and rice. Lunch sometimes lasts two hours. Afterwards, many people take a nap, called a siesta (see-ES-tah). Stores close during siesta in small towns but not in big cities.

Sports and Entertainment

Popular sports in the Dominican Republic include volleyball, basketball, and cockfighting. Cockfighting is a traditional sport brought over by the Spanish. Gamecocks look like roosters. Fans bet on which gamecock will win these fights, which usually last to the death. Some people believe it is cruel to make these animals fight each other.

Make Helado de Coco

Helado de coco is a frozen treat made from coconut milk. This delicious dessert requires no cooking. Please ask an adult to help you prepare this treat.

What You Need

Ingredients
1 14-oz (400-mL) can coconut milk
1 12-oz (354-mL) can evaporated milk
1 cup (240 mL) sugar

Equipment
can opener
medium bowl
large spoon
12 plastic or paper cups, 3 oz (88.7 mL) size
12 wooden craft spoons

What You Do

1. Mix cans of coconut and evaporated milk and sugar in a medium bowl. A mixing bowl with a pouring lip works well.
2. Pour the mixture in the plastic or paper cups, not quite to the top, and place them in the freezer.
3. After about 15 minutes, when the mixture is beginning to harden, place the craft spoons in the center of each cup.
4. Let the mixture freeze completely.
5. Serve immediately. Warm the cup in your hands to loosen the frozen mixture from the cups.

Makes 12 frozen treats

Baseball is the most popular sport in the Dominican Republic. Young boys often play stickball. Men play on amateur teams. Many professional baseball players from the Dominican Republic play on U.S. teams. Sammy Sosa and Pedro Martinez are from the Dominican Republic.

Music and Art

Many types of music are popular in the Dominican Republic, including pop, jazz, and dance. Local music is a mixture of Taíno, Spanish, and African influences. The national dance is the merengue. Merengue is fast, rhythmic music played with unique instruments. The traditional instruments are a tambora, guira, and melodeon. A tambora is a small drum with two ends. The guira is a scraping percussion instrument, and a melodeon is similar to an accordion. Today, merengue bands usually feature more than three musicians and other instruments.

Arts and crafts are popular in the Dominican Republic. Dominican paintings and sculptures are found in the country's many museums and on streetside stands. Artisans make pottery, glass religious figures, and jewelry. They also weave baskets out of palm leaves, make macramé purses, and carve wooden objects.

▼ People play a baseball game in the Dominican countryside.

The Dominican Republic's Spanish, African, and Taíno heritage continues to influence this modern, thriving country. The country has overcome past political troubles. Dominicans are hopeful that honest government will serve them as the country continues to grow and change.

▲ The merengue is the Dominican Republic's national dance.

Dominican Republic's National Symbols

◀ **Dominican Republic's Flag**
The flag is divided into four red and blue sections separated by a white cross. The blue parts represent liberty. The red parts represent the blood of people who died for freedom. The white section is a symbol of salvation. The national coat of arms lies in the center of the flag.

◀ **Dominican Republic's Coat of Arms**
The coat of arms includes a Christian Bible, a gold cross, four Dominican flags, two spears, and olive and palm branches. On a blue ribbon at the top it says, "Dios, Patria, Libertad," which means "God, Fatherland, Liberty." A red ribbon across the bottom reads Republica Dominicana.

Other National Symbols

National anthem: Himno Nacional de la Republica Dominicana (National Hymn of the Dominican Republic)

National dance: merengue

National tree: mahogany

National flower: mahogany flower

National bird: cigua palmera

Timeline

A.D. 1492
Columbus lands on the island he names Hispaniola.

1795
Spain gives its remaining land in Hispaniola to France in the Treaty of Basel.

1809
Spain again gains control of Santo Domingo.

1844
The Dominican Republic becomes independent of Haiti on February 27.

B.C.   A.D.   1700   1800

4000 B.C.
Ancestors of the Taíno migrate to the island later known as Hispaniola.

1697
The Treaty of Ryswick is signed. France then officially controls the western third of Hispaniola it had been occupying.

1801
Toussaint Louverture enters former Spanish territory to enforce the Treaty of Basel.

1822
Haiti occupies all of Hispaniola.

1916
The United States sends troops into the Dominican Republic; the troops stay for eight years.

1937
Trujillo orders people of Haitian descent in the Dominican Republic to be killed.

1965
The United States again sends troops into the Dominican Republic.

1996
Balaguer ends his last presidential term.

1950 — **2000**

1930
General Rafael Leonidas Trujillo takes power.

1961
Trujillo is assassinated.

1966
Joaquín Balaguer is elected president.

1986
Balaguer again wins presidency amid charges of election fraud.

Words to Know

amber (AM-bur)—pine sap that has hardened over millions of years into a yellowish-brown material

brujos (BROO-hohs)—witch doctors

censor (SEN-sur)—to stop free speech

corruption (kuh-RUP-shuhn)—dishonest behavior

curanderos (cur-ahn-DAY-rohs)—folk healers

fraud (FRAWD)—the practice of cheating or tricking people

free-trade zone (FREE-TRAYD ZOHN)—an area where foreign companies are not taxed on imported materials that are used to make exported products

macramé (mah-kruh-MAY)—lace or fringe made by knotting threads or cords in a geometrical pattern

merengue (may-RAYN-gay)—fast, rhythmic music traditionally played with tambora, guira, and melodeon; the merengue is also a dance.

refinery (ri-FYE-nuh-ree)—a factory where pollutants and other unwanted things are taken out of raw materials so the raw materials can be made into finished products; sugar refineries process sugarcane plants into sugar.

vodou (VOO-doo)—a religion practiced mainly by Haitians of which a Dominican version exists

To Learn More

Aller, Susan Bivin. *Christopher Columbus.* History Maker Bios. Minneapolis: Lerner, 2003.

Creed, Alexander. *Dominican Republic.* Major World Nations. Philadelphia: Chelsea House, 2000.

Howard, David John. *Dominican Republic: A Guide to the People, Politics, and Culture.* In Focus. New York: Interlink Books, 1999.

Molzahn, Arlene Bourgeois. *Sammy Sosa.* Sports Heroes. Mankato, Minn.: Capstone Press, 2001.

Moya Pons, Frank. *The Dominican Republic: A National History.* Princeton, N.J.: Markus Wiener Publishers, 1998.

Rogers, Lura, and Barbara Radcliffe Rogers. *The Dominican Republic.* Enchantment of the World. Second Series. New York: Children's Press, 1999.

Temple, Bob. *Dominican Republic.* Discovering the Caribbean. Philadelphia: Mason Crest Publishers, 2003.

Useful Addresses

Embassy of the Dominican Republic in Canada
130 Albert Street, Suite 418
Ottawa, ON K1P 5G4
Canada

Embassy of the Dominican Republic in Washington, D.C.
1715 22nd Street, N.W.
Washington, DC 20008

Internet Sites

Do you want to learn more about the Dominican Republic?
Visit the FactHound at http://www.facthound.com

FactHound can track down many sites to help you. All the FactHound sites are hand-selected by our editors. FactHound will fetch the best, most accurate information to answer your questions.

IT'S EASY! IT'S FUN!
1) Go to *http://www.facthound.com*
2) Type in: 0736821775
3) Click on "FETCH IT" and FactHound will put you on the trail of several helpful links.

You can also search by subject or book title. So, relax and let our pal FactHound do the research for you!

◀ Trujillo built this obelisk after becoming president. The obelisk has been painted several times. This painting, done in 2000, shows the Mirabal sisters who were active in a revolutionary group formed to oppose Trujillo. Three of the sisters were killed by Trujillo's police force.

Index

African culture, 45, 54, 55
African slaves, 20, 21
agriculture, 12, 16, 19, 20, 21, 37–38, 49
amber, 10
animals. See wildlife
art, 45, 54

Báez, Buenaventura, 24
Balaguer, Joaquín, 31, 32
baseball, 54, 55
Basel, Treaty of, 22
beaches, 9, 13, 16, 42
Blanco, Salvador Jorge, 32

Caribbean Sea, 6, 26
Cibao Valley, 10, 12
climate, 13–14
coat of arms, 57
Columbus, Christopher, 5, 6, 19
Columbus Lighthouse, 5–6
coral reefs, 9, 42
Cordillera Central, 9, 10, 11, 12, 14
Cordillera Septentrional, 9, 10
Cuba, 6, 19, 30

Duarte, Juan Pablo, 22–23, 24

education, 27, 34, 37, 46, 50, 51, 52
election fraud, 25, 26, 31, 32
energy, 5, 41–42
ethnic groups, 45

family life, 48–49, 50
farming. See agriculture
flag, 57
food, 37, 48, 52, 53
France, 20–21, 22, 24
free-trade zones, 38, 41

government, branches of, 33–35
Guzmán, Antonio, 31–32

Haiti, 6, 20, 22, 23, 30
health care, 34, 50
holidays, 46–47
housing, 49
hurricanes, 14

independence from Haiti, 22, 23

Jaragua National Park, 12–13

Lago Enriquillo, 12, 13, 16
livestock, 38, 49
Louverture, Toussaint, 21–22

manufacturing, 38, 49
Mella, Ramón, 22, 23, 24
mining, 20, 41
music, 54

national anthem, 57
natural resources, 39, 41
Neiba Valley, 12

Pico Duarte, 10
pirates, 20
plant life, 14, 16
Puerto Plata, 9, 42
Puerto Rico, 5, 6

religion, 46–47
Ryswick, Treaty of, 20

Saint Domingue, 20–22. See also Haiti
Samaná Peninsula, 9
Sánchez, Francisco del Rosario, 22, 23, 24
Santana, Pedro, 23–24, 25

Santiago, 10, 12
Santo Domingo, 5, 12, 14, 23, 27, 35, 42, 52
  as Spanish colony, 19, 22, 24
service industry, 37, 42
Sierra de Bahoruco, 9, 12
Sierra de Neiba, 9, 12
Spain, 19–20, 22, 24, 25, 46
Spanish culture, 45, 54, 55
sports, 52, 54

Taíno, 19, 20, 45, 54, 55
temperature, 13–14
tourism, 9, 14, 37, 42, 43
transportation, 42
Trujillo, Rafael Leonidas, 28–31, 46, 63

United States, 24, 26, 49, 52
  occupation of Dominican Republic, 26–28, 30, 31

Vásquez, Horacio, 28

War of Restoration, 24
wildlife, 12–13, 16, 17, 42